PINK TREES PRESS

"Linda Kleinbub's *Appear to Dance* is a wonderfully sensitive collection of poems. Her saving grace is her love of Nature. Linda observes birds, sycamore seeds laying on the ground, and '…waits for the evening / when the moon is high…' She tells the falcon to fly, and in her book, she does exactly that! *Appear to Dance* is a carefully-observed testament to that dark period, and it is an important one. Full of life, it will stand the test of time."
—Ron Kolm, author of *The Bookstore Book.*

"Hopeful rays shimmer through the miasma of conflict and awakening to the strength of nature budding. Kleinbub shares poems rising and falling with breath begging for confinement to end and offering the reader to join her on this journey, hands clasped in friendship and prayer. This is a must for your poetry collection."
—J R Turek, author of *DogSpeak.*

"Those of us who survived the COVID years are grateful that such a candid soul has recorded the anxiety and claustrophobia of that global pandemic–and fashioned it into crisp, daily dispatches of good poems that will show future generations how it really felt."
—Zev Shanken, *Thirty-three Poems About My Father.*

"Linda Kleinbub's exciting new volume of verse, *Appear to Dance,* chronicles life during the COVID epidemic. Her poems seemed poised on the edge of heartbreak, not an amorous one, but the social heartbreak that comes to a speaker cut off from family, gym, and, most importantly, social activities with friends. Heart-tugging moments abound, for example, the hero gives tips by phone to her son when he is sick, or when she sits like a bird among leaves in the top seats in bleachers on a deserted playing field. Reading this book, you relive those sorrowful times, re-saddening yourself with so many poignant lyrics."
—Jim Feast, author of *Karl Marx Private Eye.*

Titles from Pink Trees Press

Origami Book #1, Linda Kleinbub
Origami Book #2, Linda Kleinbub
Silver Tongued Devil Anthology,
Linda Kleinbub & Anthony C. Murphy, Editors
Poems from an Unending Pandemic, Phillip Giambri
Dysfunction: A Play on Words in the Familiar, Pauline Findlay
Good Boy, Bad Boy, A Better Man, Phillip Giambri
Naming a Hurricane, Madeline Artenberg
The Bookstore Book, Ron Kolm
Spellbook of Ordinary Mistakes, Jane LeCroy
Appear to Dance, Linda Kleinbub

For more information:
pinktreespress@gmail.com

Appear to Dance

Appear to Dance
Poems

Linda Kleinbub

Pink Trees Press
New York City

Cover Art: Linda Wulkan

Published in the United States of America by
Pink Trees Press, Inc.
Middle Village, NY 11379

First Edition 2024
ISBN: 979-8-9898695-4-1
Library of Congress Control Number:
2024936130

Notes

When the lockdown for the COVID pandemic was announced in March 2020, I sensed that we were embarking on a time of new trials and discovery. I decided to write every day. It was early spring in New York City and as an avid gardener, I was able to focus on nature's rebirth with a meticulous eye. I contracted COVID in February 2021 at a time when the vaccine was beginning to roll out and was being offered to senior citizens and members of the population who were considered "high-risk." My symptoms changed from day to day. Overall, I spent weeks in bed and feel like my health never returned to the level it was pre-COVID. Writing every day during this time allowed me to tune into the world with a conscious awareness which I believed helped me comprehend this difficult time. Thank you for reading this book and witnessing one person's pandemic experience.

Gratitude

I want to offer my heartfelt thanks to everyone who helped make this book possible:

My family, especially Konrad, who encouraged me to go to my first AWP (Association of Writers and Writing Programs) Conference in 2011 where I found "my people." Kevin, Nicholas, Jacky, and Benjamin for all the beautiful memories we share.

Thank you to my Pink Trees Press family including Phillip Giambri, Madeline Artenberg, Pauline Findlay, Linda Wulkan, Ron Kolm, and Jane LeCroy. Thank you for sharing your love, knowledge, understanding, and generosity with me. I learn something new about life and literature every time I work with you.

Barbara Henning whose workshop in person and on Zoom helped shape many poems found in this text. Judy (J R) Turek for her gifted edits and Paula Curci for all the opportunities shared with Pink Trees Press to help promote literacy.

The staff at the Writers' Colony at Dairy Hollow. The support and solitude I discovered there were life-changing and gave me the time to organize and edit this book.

The writing communities of New York City, Long Island, and Easton, Pennsylvania for providing welcoming spaces for readings and discussion.

Ultimately, I thank my Higher Power for my sobriety for without this nothing would be possible.

Thank you all for helping shape me into the writer, editor, and person I am today.

Table of Contents

LOCKDOWN 19

Pandemic 21
Corona Virus.. 22
Life Shut Down... 23
View Finder 24
Breeze Baby Blanket.................................... 25
The Fifth.. 26
Tick Tock, Tick Tock.................................... 27
A Sharp Wind Day....................................... 28
Garden Prayer 29
Runners... 30
Garden Store Chaos 31
Fordham Choir.. 32
Bright Days.. 33
Food for Thought 34
Confined 35
Out of Work... 36
The World is on Lockdown............................. 37
Bound 38
Holding the String....................................... 39
Gas Tanks Park 40
Sun On Your Skin.. 41
Heeyen's Birthday 42
Get Out of the House 43
Friday, Memorial Day Weekend 44
Monday, Memorial Day Weekend.................... 45
George Floyd 46
Riots 48
Seeking Justice... 49
Closed... 50

Three Months Home 51
Phase Two: Reopening........................... 52
Carousel.. 54
Sitting on the Bleachers......................... 55
Dance, Green, Breathe 56
Rockaway Surf... 57
What Day Is It?.. 58
The Artist's Birthday 59
Boston Road Trip.................................... 60
Muffled Conversations........................... 61
Politics in Quarantine............................ 62
The President's a Roadblock 63
Numb.. 64
Breakdown... 65
Webster's Words...................................... 66
Almost Time for Harvest......................... 67
Moonlight in the Flower Pots 68
It's Christmas Eve................................... 69
Shell Fragments 70
New Year.. 71
January 6, 2021 72
SICK WITH COVID 73

The Infiltration.. 75
This is Not Playtime................................ 76
Long Distance Healthcare 77
Symptoms: One 78
Symptoms: Two.. 79
Orifice of Digestion 80
Things Taken for Granted 82
Emerge from Hibernation....................... 83
Fairytale Princess................................... 84
Sycamore Tree.. 85
Fog of Fatigue... 86

Fahrenheit Open Mic Sunday 87
The Bird Watcher 88
The Infected One 89
Entangled Feast 90
Aftermath 91
Afterthought 92
Out After Infection 93
Coronavirus Homework 94
In the Sunlight 95
Constellations Appear to Dance 96
Welcome Home for a Lonely Soul 97
A Shot of Expectations 98
Gravity's Crush 99
Follow the Phases of the Moon 100
Saturday Afternoon 101
Sleep 102
COVID Virus 103
Acknowledgments 104
About the Author 105

For Benjamin

A virus threads its way through us, rides our blood like a subway, erasing everything.

—Nick Flynn

LOCKDOWN

Pandemic

A virus attacks the lungs
breath of life is stolen.
Congestion, pneumonia, in two weeks
death.
Everyone can be a carrier so
follow the rules.
Guidelines for survival:
handwashing often,
isolate,
just stay home,
keep a positive attitude.
Loneliness can be painful
make use of your telephone.
No one is immune.
Our cooperation is needed,
pray.
Quit procrastinating, get a chore done.
Remember:
spring is a new beginning.
Tulips push through dirt
unearthing chlorophyll.
Value the gifts of
water and earth.
X-amine the entire picture—
yellow sun will rise tomorrow
zebras are still black and white.

Corona Virus

Communicable disease in
our congested city
relegates us to stay home.
Originated in Wuhan, China—
now spread across the Earth
a virus, a deadly disease.

Virtual connections,
isolation for those living alone—
remembering simpler days.
Unless we stay separated
sickness will continue.

Life Shut Down

Loneliness is wrapped around New York City
sheltering in place
your muscles are tight
you're grinding your teeth.

All the bars and restaurants shut down.
Scores of corned beef and green beer
never made it to market.
All the cafés and pubs shut down.

Five weeks since non-essential businesses
closed. My gym, the library,
the church holy doors—all shuttered.
Five weeks since meetings were banned;

my fellowship, my therapist unable to meet.
Healing love has shut down.
We are told to stay home; what have we done?
The Earth is in bloom–pink flowers in trees.

I seek comfort in tulip petals and dandelions–
photographing the Earth's rebirth
tending to the garden.
Five weeks since life has shut down.

View Finder

Wandering, camera in hand,
I photograph flowering trees

bursting buds pink and white.
I try to forget the news

strolling in solitude.
I photograph blue jays jeering

songbirds perched in trees
crouching to capture daffodils' bloom.

A bumble bee finds crocus nectar
as Earth begins to hum again.

Bright green leaves sprout from trees.
Most people stay indoors.

Quiet streets bring clean air.
Mother Nature calms my nerves.

Breeze Baby Blanket

Breeze baby blanket caressing softly my skin
spring bursts into pastel pink and sunny hues

time to tend the garden
awake her from a slumbered berth

blackberry vines wildly scatter
time to trim the dead branches

old wood now feeds the fire
tie back the new runners

green vines
twisted in the dance

along the fence they arabesque
stretch high, then curve low

songbird melodies fill the air
breeze baby blanket caressing softly my skin

The Fifth

I find solace next to a radio
playing a tune
I know by heart.

My horoscope predicts
fear in an unknown future
loss of home, humanity.

Radio songs
sing my troubles
caress me with melody.

It's cold and rainy.
The businessman announces,
"It's the fifth week on Zoom

soon people will begin to crack.
Let's incorporate a virtual happy hour
join in with the drink of your choice."

Tick Tock, Tick Tock

Wake up busy
laundry, coffee, internet
tick tock, tick tock
a phone call from Kentucky

as I'm talking to a lawyer
my partner says, "Stay out of my way."
Check on the laundry, my coffee is cold
my stomach is agitated

Go for a walk
begin to unwind
look up to see cottony clouds
start noticing tulips and jays

Walk along the highway
cross Eliot Avenue to Juniper Valley Park
photograph pink and white trees:
cherries, pears, magnolias, and dogwoods

I can keep busy creating distractions
or just sit, breathe,
marvel at the clouds
and think about you

A Sharp Wind Day

Cotton balls soaked in gray paint
hang heavy in the sky, a chilly dampness
freezes exposed fingers and toes
holiday plans merge, converge, emotions surge

Disconnected from practices of faith
socially distanced apart
erases connections once felt
family dinners replaced by funeral masses

Nature's rebirth of first crocus blooms
bright yellow ruffled daffodils
strive to bring springtime cheer—
winter's persistence drains colors to white

Mother Nature's April fool
We are all wearing masks
singing is not allowed in church
I'm still hoping to find harmony

Garden Prayer

A radio plays bluesy rock.
I'm sitting in my garden
looking for hope.
I've been saved from my fiery fate.
It's been 800 days
since my last drink.
Now, home alone—
trying to keep the faith.

So hard to keep the demons away
when the church doors are locked
and the choir's gone away.
I water plants with my tears
when I focus my eyes, I see peppermint grow.
I think of you as I wonder
if you thanked your guardian angel today,
and I pray.

Runners

A sparrow's song fills the sky
between us, a six-foot fence
filters the afternoon sun.
My neighbor Patty and I talk about runners—
we shout through the white-plastic-privacy
slats, socially isolating for so long.

This end of April balmy day
we talk of bluebirds in the flowering pear tree,
cardinals too. So many more birds
since Corona came to town.
We walk along the fence,
a chain-link barrier between us.

I'm pulling at the branches
crossing the property line.
"Don't cut them down. They thrive in our soil.
Let them burst into bud, white blossoms
will transform into sweet juicy fruit."
I let her know, "They're blackberries."

Garden Store Chaos

I carry an empty propane tank
looking for a refill
people wearing masks
buying plants
I spot a sparrow in the thicket
cruising bread crumbs tossed his way
I've been feeling very lonely
living in the year of just-stay-home

It started with a quiet click
of a closing door
The days the lights in bars and
restaurants went dark
People we knew began getting sick
People we knew were dying
We stayed home and
counted the caskets on TV

Flowers began to bloom
I photographed colors
now all is green
The soil is warm, ready to till
time to get in gear
time to plant tomatoes and beans
some hot peppers, too
Time to start planting once more

Fordham Choir

I find peace on public radio.
Connections once felt
prayers of promise

lighting votive candles
fade each day away.
Under an awning of silver clouds

purple flowers once glowed—
bright lights among green leaves.
I meditate at nature's altar.

Bright Days

Avalanche of feelings
blows me down.
Carcass found roadside
decays.
Evolution changes everything.
Fossil fuels found at
gas pumps.
Hydrangeas are dwarfed by
irises blooming.
Jellybeans mail-ordered
kept in my pocket.
Living in isolation,
marking time in
nowhere land. I'll avoid
opium dens and
prison cells.
Quarantine life is a trap—
rescue me.
Turning a new leaf,
understand
vegetable gardens need
water to thrive. I'll plant a
xyst to shade the
yellow sun and
zinnias embodying friendship.

Food for Thought

First time to Northside Bakery
since lockdown began

six weeks ago.
Outside, customers line up

four to six feet apart.
I wait behind

a Polish-speaking family,
mom, dad, teen, and grade school daughters

wear black latex gloves
and surgical masks.

The teen starts coughing.
I begin to worry.

Is it worth dying for a
good loaf of bread?

Confined

Brisk wind brings a chill
fifty-three days without you
my flesh needs your touch

Out of Work

I haven't been to the gym in three months.
My intense exercise regime
of nearly twenty years has halted.
I'm told to stay home and I do.

There's no entertainment–
bars, restaurants, Broadway, cabarets,
strip clubs, concert halls, sports arenas,
gyms, libraries, shopping malls–

everything is closed.
There are hunger lines, unemployment lines.
Life has ceased.
Nature continues to evolve without us.

My body is falling into my skin,
my bones are collapsing inside me,
my hair is falling out.
I'm aging faster than the sundial.

The World is on Lockdown

We are sheltering in place.
Grandma Bridie is now 90.

She lives alone baking Irish soda bread
and chocolate chip cookies.

Before the virus, we shopped in supermarkets.
We gathered together without fear.

Now we are told to stay home,
but when you live alone,

especially in your senior years,
isolation becomes an ugly monster.

Without technology:
no Facebook,

no Instagram or TikTok to view,
no Zoom conferencing to connect you,

the isolation monster feeds on loneliness.
Crawling out of the TV at night

he begins to gnaw on Grandma.
The family that comforts her

is told to avoid her.
She finds it hard to understand, why.

A frightened child calls out in the night,
"I'm out in the rain! Where are you?"

Bound

I'm holding onto my last breath
as lilacs blow away

Searching discomforting clouds
branches grabbing for attention

Once a bare bush
now leaves cover branches

My feet are stuck in concrete
life in a box

Holding the String

Going through the motions
getting chores done

I'm trapped / I'm free
fighting a war at home

My feet are stuck in concrete
I'm looking at the clouds

Floating puffs of white and grey
sunset orange warms me

I can't get out
I'm looking for a cure

holding a string
let the kite fly me free

Gas Tanks Park

Answering emails that are
backlogged for days,
clear the electronic clutter
darkening your path.
Evolve as the Earth revolves,
frolicking along the way.
Gently tread along the
highway, cross the overpass to
investigate Gas Tanks Park.
Journey to bluebells and cherry blossoms.
Keep a safe distance
living in isolated city.
Modern-day medicine man
never saw this coming.
Only God knows how it will end.
People are dying, as we live in
quarantine.
Relax, if you can.
Solitude is unseen
torment.
Under house arrest, we are innocent of
violations of the law. We
work to reduce this plague's
xeroxing abilities.
Yearning for human interaction while
zooming for recovery.

Sun On Your Skin

Sun on your skin
laundry drying in the sky

scans of origami causing paper jams
and reboots

Birthday parties
without cutting a cake

Jubilation in isolation
wave from your window, as cars go by

Children throw candy at your stoop
Balloons fly from car windows into tree branches

Join me for a virtual celebration
Another day home

safe
fed
protected

Heeyen's Birthday

Celebration plans
send gifts without leaving home
mailbox surprises

Zoom birthday party
virtual festivities
internet laughter

Far, though I see you
grateful for years of friendship
Happy Birthday, Girl

Digital birthday
celebrate with me online
too far to taste cake

Get Out of the House

Are you using your time the
best way possible?
Clicking clocks keep ticking
days go by, seasons change on
Earth. Winter
frost thawed to
green, continues growing.
Human touch is now a memory,
interactions limited.
"Just stay home" will
keep us close to family or
let isolation
melt into your
nerves.
Open the door and let your
pores begin to breathe.
Questions will continue to
rise from sun up to
sunset. Look past the
trapped mentality.
Understand you can still seek
virtue, serenity is possible.
Wake to the new morning light.
Xylophone's tune may startle you.
Zip up your jacket, get out of the house.

Friday, Memorial Day Weekend

Memorial Day
quarantine, parades canceled
traditions halted

Monday, Memorial Day Weekend

Home alone for the first time
since solitary confinement began
my shoulders are relaxed

I blast the radio
on every floor of the house—
finally, freedom!

A rock and roll party in my garden
as the sound of music
pours out of the windows and doors

George Floyd

On the last Monday of May
we live in lockdown
spring blooms into Memorial Day

the unofficial kick-off to summer.
We are all anxious, we are all tense
living in solitary loneliness until

INJUSTICE!
George Floyd
an unarmed black man is killed

by a white policeman.
George Floyd was murdered
by police officer Derek Chauvin

by pressing his knee
into his neck.
Caught on video

white supremacy
gun violence, bigotry, hatred, racism.
We are living incarcerated

we are all restless.
Now we have a tragedy
we cry out

call for justice.
The pot has been bubbling
now the fire has been ignited.

Innocent people get hurt
hatred breeds hatred
manifested in darkness.

Seek peace
seek tolerance
seek understanding
seek knowledge
seek love.

Riots

Walking for exercise
to help relieve stress
a bench to rest at the
Quick Brown Fox Triangle Park.

I check my phone to see reports of looting
at the Queens Center Mall.
A Facebook post says after looting the mall
there are plans to attack my neighborhood.

Trump's hate and racism has festered–
it oozes through MAGA's minds.
A peaceful existence
I once took for granted—
no more.

Seeking Justice

Atmospheric pressure
barometers rising
cataclysmic events
drag us into reality.
Evergreen forests
filled with pine
generate a bed of soft needles.
Hills and mountains
invite you to
journey with me.
Kindness heals wounds.
Love unites.
More work is needed
now with greater reason.
Organized
protesters march daily.
Questions
remain.
Screaming voices
together
unite for
victory. Hoping these actions
will be
xeroxed
yielding
zero tolerance.

Closed

Is it exhaustion from lack of living?
Or exhaustion from exercise and laundry?

Words wander from your mouth
reach the ears of innocent listeners

the world's in chaos
worldwide pandemic

New York City shutdown
businesses closed for months

skyrocketing unemployment
rampant gunfire echoes in the streets

an innocent man killed
social unrest

schools are planning to open soon
children in classrooms

courthouses remain closed
criminals go free

Three Months Home

Three months since life shut down.
Seclusion smacked in–
stayed like a sloth.

Revolving in a bubble, some daytime activity,
dinner, TV, bedtime.
What day is it anyway?

Internet video gatherings provide
meetings and readings,
you can virtually travel the land.

But can you stand?
Have you ridden a subway?
Are you ready to?

We gather together in Brady Bunch squares
Zoom conferencing. Let me peek into your life
check out your bookshelves and

your bric-a-brac.
Let's meet your children and your pets.
We assemble together on virtual stages

hear me, hear me
see me, see me
but can anybody feel me?

Phase Two: Reopening

Phase two of the reopening
of New York began today.
Are you wearing a mask?
Please don't leave home without one.

The mayor says, "Step right up
We're open for business—
outdoor dining and haircuts
right this way."

The city is empty
the rich have fled
to the Hamptons and the Berkshires;
the techies are all working from home.

New York City is undergoing
a transformation before my eyes
civil unrest
a president who lies

injustice in the streets
responded to by looting and protests
gun violence is rampant
as protestors shout "Defund the Police!"

Life shut down in March
but when the lid is locked
and the pressure cooker heats up,
it's inevitable that it will explode.

Phase two of the reopening of New York—
Are you ready to eat on the sidewalks
of the gritty city?
Do you fear contact and wish to stay home?

Are you getting your haircut?
Touching up your color?
Are you ready to go shopping again?
The doors are open at Bloomingdale's

and The Gap.
Will the open mic return?
Will we congregate in concert halls
with throngs in celebration cheering as one?

Not too likely
anytime soon.

Carousel

She wants to live an honest life
it's so hard you know.
He provides fuel to sustain her
holds her to absorb her pain
living sequestered since March.

Now the sturgeon moon shines
she is slowly dying inside.
Her bones are falling into her skin
collapsing into herself.
She's losing her sex drive.

Lack of participation
lack of exercise
lack of mental stimulation
world of confinement
days blur together
as paint peels from ceilings.

Ticking of time
life exists on Zoom in her few rooms
connection electronic
Facebook distraction
a spectacle of illusion.
Everybody's struggling, you know?
She's not a singer,
but the joy of singing with others
in a concert arena is gone.
Quarantine, how much longer
must she live with you?

Sitting on the Bleachers

Wind blows through me
pulls my hair to cover my eyes.
Left of me
roller-skating boys smack hockey sticks,
bikers fly by.
Baseball field before me,
empty field—a quiet sound.
The pitcher's mound has worn to the ground.

Wind continues to play with my hair.
Wind blows through me.
Overhead the peach leaves
shush with wind.

Who's wiser?
Peachtree next to me
will probably live longer.
Knows how to survive
swaying in sunshine.
Relaxes deep down into its roots
holds firmly to the Earth
allows itself to be fed
by the grace of rain.

Peachtree, teach me how to live
keep me planted
swaying in the sunshine.
Wind blows through me.
I listen, planted, grow.

Dance, Green, Breathe

> I am the Lorax;
> I speak for the trees.
> —Dr. Seuss

I'm still learning.
I seek wisdom from trees.
I climb to the top shady corner
of the little league bleachers.
I am leaf level.
Hideaway in the park
breeze reminds me of other things.
Facetime friend's plans begin to emerge.
Good to see you in person again,
even on a tiny screen.
We're still in isolation, loneliness
grows in dried grass on empty playfields.

Making plans to travel during a pandemic
requires a good cancellation policy
should the virus spike.
Research what attractions are still closed.
There's always the waterfront
open-air distractions of a park
trying to break the hum-drum dailies.
I climb to the top of the Little League bleachers
to be oak-leaf level.
Silent in their story whispering
secrets of longevity:
stay planted, rooted in your space
don't try to stop the wind.
Let your body sway
dance, green, breathe.

Rockaway Surf

The beach is crowded
boogie boarders ride the waves

toddlers use shovels and pails
to dig sand holes until water appears

sandcastles topple, seashells line the shoreline
jingle bells signal the ice cream cart

seagulls search the sand
for remnants left by surfers.

Forget coronavirus momentarily–
warm your body in the sun

What Day Is It?

It's July two? I thought it was three.
Who's keeping track anymore?
July 4th is on a Saturday

perfect day for this holiday
get out in the sun
celebrate America

barbeque with friends
but we're still living with COVID.
It's July two? I thought it was three.

Who's keeping track anymore?
Confinement is a lonely scene.
Eating California Rolls alone

I think of what you're going through.
I stop, and begin to cry
my body shakes

curls into my skeleton
salty tears flow into my mouth
I lose my appetite.

July Fourth no red, white, and blue.
Pandemic persistence,
when will you be through?

The Artist's Birthday

For Linda Wulkan

Division Street, Chinatown
Picnic umbrellas provide shade
for a circle of friends
clinking glasses for the birthday girl.
Outdoor diners, wearing masks,
shifting folding chairs to avoid the sun.
A thunderstorm rolls in
blasting wind driving rain sideways
claps of thunder, bright lightning
scuttling party guests venture
into the bar turned general store.
The barkeep ushers the group
to the stay-dry backroom
against all social distancing rules.
They gather together
sing birthday songs
eat caramel cake
while keeping a few feet apart.
Wearing a mask except for sipping and eating.
The drinks flowed
alcohol is sure to kill the germs.
Friends gathering
for the first time in four months
trying to act normal
celebrating a birthday
in quarantine.

Boston Road Trip

For Jada

"I go to B.U. I'm Katie.
My friend Mia plays soccer there."
Captain Scott's Lobster Dock,

Friday afternoon,
mist of ending rainstorm
lingers along the highway.

Straight ride on I-95
driving free at 70 miles per hour.
A friendly stranger sets the tone—

you're safe among friends.
Escape from New York
locked down for so long.

Freedom trails are yours to explore.
Lessons learned—
to dine dockside, reservations are needed.

Follow the electronic navigation Google
or follow the landmark bright lights.
We discover a land of revelations,

as we journey through the Commons.
Make way for the ducklings!
Make way for the Geminis!

Muffled Conversations

Back to school sighs found
in the brisk August air.
Will the children be safe?

What will they learn?
This mixed-up world where it's deemed
safe to educate children indoors

but unsafe for adults
to break a sweat at the gym.
Indoor dining is available in Nassau County

a quick drive from Queens.
Only outdoor dining in the city.
There's still so much confusion

about this infection—
unreliable test results.
Each day we grow older

the ticking of time
a funeral to bury loved ones
a wedding with hopes for a happy union.

We wear masks
muffled conversations, an elbow bump
we gather without hugs or kisses.

Politics in Quarantine

If I told you a story about a president
afraid he will lose re-election

so, he took all the mailboxes away.
You might think that sounds like fiction

but this day we live
a continuous Groundhog Day.

New Yorkers are fleeing the city
gunfire has replaced

Independence Day fireworks.
Unemployment is high

as businesses continue to close.
Democratic/ Republican conventions begin

a virtual spectacle, without audience fanfare.
Empty theaters as delegates take the stage

while mailboxes are removed from the streets,
mail sorting machines whisked away.

Our president tries to stop the mail
to prevent voter's tallies.

The President's a Roadblock

Forty days until election day
on your way to the voting machines
what do you see?
Hunger lines,

unemployment lines,
people wearing masks
our children shuffle through
bureaucratic educational stumbling blocks.

My hometown is breaking down—
gunfire rapidly takes lives
of infants and fathers.
TikTok, TikTok

the president's a roadblock.
Seven months in confinement.
Our president can't serve the nation
he's running on lies. It's obscene.

Numb

Do you numb yourself
to stop yourself from thinking?

Are you afraid to allow yourself
the life you need?

Living in a holding cell
you get on my nerves.

Go through the motions
living in bubbles day by day.

Are you brave enough
to continue the journey alone?

Fireworks explode
in nights of civil unrest.

Breakdown

My body is breaking down
it's been five months

since my gym closed
before shutdown

I exercised for nineteen years
three to four times a week

Summer's heavy humidity and
burning heat limits my movement

I'm slowing down
My shoulders are collapsing

I struggle to stay active
For now, dancing to the radio

softens my muscles
awakens my bones

Webster's Words

Black-eyed Susans stand petalless
dark sienna seed balls
upon thin stems

Autumn has begun
season to prepare for winter
it's been seven months

since quarantine began
"Zoom Fatigue" and "Zoom Bombing"
added to the dictionary

A flock of sparrows
rises in the air startled

Almost Time for Harvest

Almost time for harvest in my
backyard vegetable garden.
Creation of a focal point
during quarantine. My
energy shifted to tending
fragile seedlings,
growing pole beans
hot wiri wiri peppers.
I contemplate my lessons learned
juggling home life and Zoom.
Kids are missing out on
lessons learned.
More than seven months with
no clear answers.
October 24th, elections begin. The
political fiasco will
quickly escalate
rising to a
shrieking pitch.
Time will decide the
United States' future, I've hope of
victory for the people
with liberty and justice for all.
X-amine your heart before
you vote, so hopefully, the chaos of the current
zoo will come to order.

Moonlight in the Flower Pots

She waits for the evening
when the moon is high to sit outside
in her little backyard
next to the flowering pear tree
She seeks silence, listens to the wind
In the distance an ambulance speeds by
Someone is shooting fireworks
into the cloudy damp sky

She looks into the treetops, lace-like grace
Time alone in the quiet city
cars hum on the highway nearby
She's been going through the motions
trying to focus on the positive good
She seeks strength with pullies and weights
still, her body decays
lack of movement, stagnation

No fun in a concert hall or baseball stadium
she has stayed home so many months
Now the holidays are on hold—
a trying time
Tomorrow turkey's stuffing begins
in a hot skillet with melted butter and sage
Moonlight in the flower pots
the rosemary glows green

It's Christmas Eve

It's been a challenging year
tension was brewing on the kitchen counter

After another debacle
I lost it

I screamed and stomped my feet
behavior of yesterday's days

Darkest time on Earth
the wall between us has grown

Neil Young's *Harvest Moon*
reminds me

I'm still in love with you
I want to see you dance again.

Shell Fragments

As I emerge from my shell
fragments crack away
I feed myself blueberries
flown in from Peru

As it snows a curtain of
fine floating ice crystals
in the land where I live
forest bare branches ground cover thick

crackling red, yellow leaves
dried brown on the forest floor
Leaves once the source of
chlorophyll green life

create a soft place for my footsteps
First snow a silent surprise
frosty flakes floating through the silver sky
tree's limbs leafless catch snowdrops

covered in an outline of pure white
The Inuit people call it Qali
I'm in awe at Mother Nature
grateful to be in New York City this December

New Year

The New Year comes in silent air
scented sachets of lavender calm

stillness for a moment, to reflect and carry hope
This night lit with Christmas lights

in multicolored hues
a cold moon sky

The constellation galaxy carries
Gemini and Mars tonight

New Year's midnight
fireworks light the heavens

Flashes of diamond sparkles
lines of glowing color in view

January 6, 2021

Refusing to accept he lost the election
the president calls to arms his supporters:
evangelical Christians, white supremacists,

the Proud Boys, and the Oath Keepers
they storm the Capitol
with guns, pepper spray, and baseball bats.

Our president is unstable
blinded by the orange glow of his hair.
There is no peaceful transfer of power—

with prejudice and the devil's fear
delusional wildfire scorches the Earth.
Refusing reality,

refusing sanity—
truth and justice,
where did it go?

SICK WITH COVID

The Infiltration

It's too late
creeping into my organs
the virus, deadly to mankind
Infection causes severe fatigue
drugs can help the achiness and pain

This is Not Playtime

Like dominos lined up
ready to topple
COVID creeps and conquers

from a father to a son to a mother to a friend
500,000 Americans gone
How many survived with side effects?

Today a new strain develops
Who's next?
When do the dominos stop falling?

Long Distance Healthcare

The virus affects people differently–
possible symptoms are varied and many

Today my son has it in his lungs
I send him homemade remedies

ginger tea, eucalyptus, and Vicks vapor rub
long distance healthcare

leaves me in fear for him
I turn to God

Symptoms: One

COVID hits me with body pain
cramping in my back and hips
overcome by fatigue
I lay in bed most of the day
with cats by my side.

Symptoms: Two

One week has passed since I first felt faint
felled by fatigue

I awake to less body pain, more energy
discover I've lost taste and smell

My morning coffee is watery and weak
I apologize for not making a proper pot

But you assure me it's rich and robust
My breakfast is texture, not flavor

uneven crunchiness of cereal
smooth consistency of yogurt

I register missing
sweetness of honey,

vanilla of yogurt,
tartness of cherries

I hardly notice the pungent eucalyptus
of Vicks on my chest

Orifice of Digestion

Loss of taste
my tongue useless for savoring flavors
coffee is acidic water
My feast is textures
taste is a tingling sensation
of citrus on my tongue

another symptom today
Every day of sickness I nap
My symptoms morph
twist my spine
It's Sunday night, one week since
I began to feel the effects of

this virus in my body
Energy levels fluctuate day by day
The last few nights trouble sleeping
taking Melatonin to slumber
Today I awaken feeling refreshed
I attempt a load of laundry

Yearning for breakfast,
scrambled eggs, toast, OJ on the side too
By 1 pm the bed is most welcoming
I sleep with cats until past four

In quarantine for at least two more days
When will the Health Department end

their daily phone calls?
Will I be strong enough?
Will I be healed?
Will I ever be able to walk,
shop, exercise again?
I pray strength comes to me

to fight this disease
antibodies born to me
attack these culprits within me
Let me be free from Corona
Let me be free
Let me be free

Things Taken for Granted

For the first time in a week
I was able to put on socks
without having to lie on my back
with my feet in the air
because of the stiffness and sharp
pain in my hips

Emerge from Hibernation

Crawling out of the cocoon
emerging towards sunlight
lethargic muscles begin to soften.

Breathing deep to clear my lungs.
Longing for the day
when antibodies will dance

in my bloodstream.
Makes me wonder
if a vaccination is necessary.

Fairytale Princess

COVID crisis sends my friend to the hospital
A phone call in distress

they want to put her on a respirator
My symptoms lingering fatigue,

needing afternoon naps, congestion,
loss of taste and smell

March begins today
approaching one year of solitary confinement

Rapunzel locked away in my tower
peering out the upstairs window

I see you in the yard below
My tower built of infectious disease

Trapped, I dare not let my hair down
Please know that I miss you

isolated in my loneliness
petals in the wind

Sycamore Tree

It's been twelve days
since I first felt sick
I'm still tired, leaning toward a nap

I walk to Juniper Tennis Court Playground
to sit and take in spring
Margie has pneumonia

I pass through the empty ballfields
the earth has softened from melted snowpack
under the tall sycamore

pointy jagged seeds try to twist my ankles
through my boots they poke the soles of my feet
my steps uneven

sycamore seeds spiked balls
scattered around the trunk
decorate the ground for me

sycamore seeds littering the ground
waiting, hoping to grow up
become a tree

Fog of Fatigue

My reflexes are slow
loss of smell and taste
challenges of thirst
citrus tingle
spicy stings

Acrid airborne goes down sweet
Nap with cats till mid-afternoon then sit
get some typing done
In oxygenated hospital rooms
my friend struggles on steroids to breathe

As we count the friends and relatives
in the graveyard
recovery comes slowly
if you're lucky
with side effects still unknown

Fahrenheit Open Mic Sunday

She walks away from the camera
takes off her blue velvet jacket
places it back on its soft hanger

With a baby-oil-soaked cotton ball
she removes thick layers of mascara
white cotton rounds

transform to black
Washing her face with warm water and Dove
she looks in the mirror to reveal

sleepy eyes, saggy skin
she can fight fatigue no more
An afternoon nap for two and a half hours

was needed before going on Zoom
She's still in a slow stupor
lacking smell always

lacking taste some of the time
She's healing slowly
as she prays for her hospitalized friend

The Bird Watcher

Naked trees against a cerulean sky
reaching branches glow sunlit
dark lace along the blue horizon

Falcon circles overhead
wide white wingspan
catches my eye

Falcon sees more than my view
Sixteen days since I first felt sick
I'm looking for adventure

Flight discovery lifts my spirits
time to slowly get back to tempo
Falcon fly, let me soar

The Infected One

I return to the Little League bleachers
find a seat in the sunniest spot
It's the first balmy day this winter

One year since the plague arrived
The park is active, tennis courts are full
children climb the jungle gym

Dog walkers gather for a sniff and meet
about half wear masks
some people sit alone masked

while some groups meet unmasked
The vaccine has been rolled out
new guidelines from the CDC

Alone, I walk, my mask at my chin
I raise it whenever I pass someone
not taking any chances now

not sure I'm truly healthy
I've seen how quickly transmission occurs
I'm protecting the rest of the world from me

Entangled Feast

Snowpack has melted
earth is wet and soft
bulbs awaken from their frosty slumber
push green toward sunlight

Weather patterns shift
South wind warms
light lengthens as dawn shines to daybreak
forces deep underground emerge

past the army of beetles and worms
entangled feast, we rise to the sunrise
recycle life's cycle, start anew
organic and pure

Aftermath

Morning rising sun is shining
a pot of hot coffee awaits me
I survived coronavirus

morning Zoom therapy
an invitation to Boog City
raking the garden clear of twigs and leaves

forecast the symphony of daffodils and tulips
The ground is thawing, emerging expectation
earthen plot cleared, let the green breathe

Stroll to the store for ingredients for dinner
cooking in the early afternoon
browning beef in the pressure cooker

chopping vegetables while making phone calls
a shower with soothing relief
self-care with Dove and body scrub

Confined to home during illness
I have to tell myself it's a good day
but I'm still worried about you in the hospital

hooked up to oxygen and intravenous tubes
A tasty dinner, then a comedy film
time to reflect watching smoke rings again

Afterthought

One year since the pandemic struck
got sick as spring began

Rebirth is shadowed by lingering clouds
purple crocuses seem faded

Lost in a fog
infected by not wearing a mask

thought I was safe
My symptoms started with hip and back pain

Out After Infection

A trip to Lexington Ear, Nose, and Throat
prescription prednisone, Dymista
another coronavirus test too
My friend is freed from the hospital
returning home to nurture her cure

I escape to a fantasy fling
back to reality
the winds are shifting
COVID haze still surrounds me
worn out by worry of repercussions

an outing without a mask
a ripple of illness grows into infinity
Vaccinations are being administered
efficiently as possible
as antibodies accumulate in my bloodstream

Coronavirus Homework

Smelling is limited
things I don't smell
even though I know they have an odor:

cat litter
body odor
oranges

Dr. Stackpole E.N.T. specialist
assigns smelling homework
to reconnect my senses to my brain

In the Sunlight

In the sunlight
warmth penetrates my skin
a breeze blows through me

as I inhale and exhale
listening closer to sparrow's song
whistles and chirps

rumbles of a distant highway
children's laughter
causes my mind to wander

slows down the panic
You're allowed to have fun
Do you remember how to play?

Run around the park
ride a swing
try to fly

Constellations Appear to Dance

One month living with coronavirus
am I healed?

Prescription bottles are empty
follow up next week

clear head, lungs hopefully too
Smoke lifts like clouds

rising into the starry midnight-blue sky
half-moon floating in outer space

constellations appear to dance
my nose is cold

I'll bathe in warm lavender
crawl in bed beside you

wrap my body around you
our universe

Welcome Home for a Lonely Soul

Before the overwhelming
undercurrents pull her through
reefs, tumbling, nauseous confusion
overtakes her reach
Under her skin
her nerves trembling

She works on a project
loses sleep stays up late
sends emails
Exhaustion replaces excitement
she withdraws

There was no promise ring
Was it the toll of disease on her body
or the toll of a year in quarantine
that changed her?

What does she want?
A welcome home
for a lonely soul

A Shot of Expectations

Another gray morning, achy joints, a blasé head
Hearing a second vaccine relieves long COVID

I search the internet for Pfizer
after a few misdirected results showing

Moderna and Johnson's & Johnson's
I discover my local Walgreens

has two open appointments
A shot in my arm at 4 pm

yields little soreness
so far, not much more

Gravity's Crush

I have to learn to carry my bones
like a mobile hanging from a string

from my head to my spine
Gravity pulls my shoulders round

weight of skull
crushes organs

Learning to stand straight
string lifts my head

allows my heart to rise
Chest uplifted

shoulders fall to grace
in place

Follow the Phases of the Moon

She wasn't sure of the direction
the ground was wet dirt

uneven patches of grass
She tried to take a direct route

avoiding the winding concrete path
She searched the constellations

followed the phases of the moon
Looking up, she was lost in the woods

getting snagged by bramble
trudging through the thicket

her destination uncertain
holding her breath

Searching the night sky
she traveled

found a clearing
built a simple shelter

laid her head on the earth
to watch the wind

carry the clouds
covering moonlight

Saturday Afternoon

Cat walks through keyboard
interferes with Zoom call
dinnertime is near

Sleep

Silence the jitterbug
let yourself rest
Evening's herbal tea
entices you to dream
Put yourself in bed

COVID Virus

Children, what will you
observe, what will you remember?
Valuable lessons are not
identified in classrooms.
Designate responsibility.

Virus kills humans, cleans Earth.
Inside every torment is a
reason to survive.
Understand, I don't have answers but I'll
share all my knowledge for a cure.

Acknowledgments

Grateful acknowledgment is made to the editors of the following publications where these poems have appeared:
"Bright Days," *The Scene Zine September 2024*
"COVID Virus," *brevitas 20 2023 Anthology*
"Dance, Green, Breathe," *Home Planet News Issue 8*
"Food for Thought," *The COVID Poetry Files*
"Heeyen's Birthday," *The COVID Poetry Files*
"Get Out of the House," *27th Annual Poetry Ink Anthology*
"Pandemic," *The COVID Poetry Files*
"Politics in Quarantine," *MAINTENANT 18: A Journal of Contemporary Dada Writing and Art, 2024*
"Saturday Afternoon," *The COVID Poetry Files*
"Sitting on the Bleachers," *Poets of Queens 2 Anthology 2024*
"Sleep," *First Literary Review East* May/June 2024
"The Artist's Birthday," *Home Planet News Issue 8*
"The Fifth," *Home Planet News Issue 8*
"The World is On Lockdown," *Here We Are (A Rhapsody in View): ANYDSWPE 2024 Anthology*
"View Finder," *Riverside Poets Anthology Volume 20*
"What Day is It?" *Home Planet News Issue 8*

brevitas 20 2023 Anthology, edited by Ron Kolm & Steve Zeitlin, published by brevitas, 2023
The COVID Poetry Files, edited by Evie Ivy, published by Ra Rays Press, 2023
Here We Are (A Rhapsody in View): ANYDSWPE 2024 Anthology, edited by C.D. Johnson, published by Rogue Scholars Press, 2024
MAINTENANT 18: A Journal of Contemporary Dada Writing and Art, edited by Peter Carlaftes and Kat Georges, published by Three Rooms Press, 2024
Moonstone Arts Center –27th Poetry Ink Anthology published by Moonstone Arts, 2024
Poets of Queens 2 Anthology, edited by Jared Beloff & Olena Jennings, published by Poets of Queens Press, 2024
Riverside Poets Volume 20, edited by Norma Levy, published by Riverside Poets Press, 2022

Nick Flynn, excerpt from "Memento Mori" from Some Ether. Copyright © 2000 by Nick Flynn. Reprinted with the permission of The Permissions Company, LLC on behalf of Graywolf Press, Minneapolis, Minnesota, graywolfpress.org.

About the Author

Linda Kleinbub is the Founding Editor of Pink Trees Press, the curator of Fahrenheit Open Mic, and the co-founder of Pen Pal Poets. She's the author of *Cover Charge* (Autonomedia, 2022) and co-editor of *Silver Tongued Devil Anthology* (Pink Trees Press, 2020.) Linda was one of six local poets invited to read at the Americas Poetry Festival of New York 2021. She's been a mentor, contributing editor, and committee member at Girls Write Now. She's a member of the literary collectives brevitas and the Unbearables. She's published in *Best American Poetry, The Observer, The Brooklyn Rail,* and various journals and anthologies. She received her Master's in Fine Art in Creative Writing from The New School. She is a native New Yorker, born, raised, and still resides in Queens.

www.ingramcontent.com/pod-product-compliance
Lightning Source LLC
Chambersburg PA
CBHW071530120626
46550CB00006B/2406